HOPES and FEARS

HOPES and FEARS

PAST and PRESENT

by Peter W. Petschauer

OTHER PUBLICATIONS BY THE AUTHOR:

A Perfect Portrait,
A Novel about an 18th Century
German Woman Painter
(Charleston, 2016)

In the Face of Evil.
The Sustenance of Traditions.
(Charleston, 2014)

Der Vater und die SS.
(Brixen/Bessanone, IT, 2007)

Human Space:
Finding Our Place
in a Threatening World.
(Greenwood Press, 1997)

The Language of History:
A Topical Approach
to World Civilization.
(Dubuque, 1990)

The Education of Women
in 18th Century Germany:
Bending the Ivy.
(Lewisburg, 1989)

Afers, Gedanken zur Geschichte.
(Brixen/Bressanone, IT, 1985)

*Dedicated
to Joni Webb Petschauer,
my wife of 36 years,
my true love,
friend,
and
companion.*

Published in 2019 by the
MindMend Publishing Co., New York, NY

Copyright © 2018 by Peter Petschauer

All rights reserved.

For permissions to reproduce more than 100 words of this publication, email to ORIPressEditor@gmail.com or write to MindMend Publishing Editor @ 7515 187th St, Fresh Meadows, NY 11366.

Printed in the United States of America on acid free paper.

Library of Congress Control Number: 2018968330

Cataloging Data:

Petschauer, Peter. Hopes and Fears: Past and Present / Peter Petschauer

1. Poetry. 2. Psychobiography. 3. Psychohistory. 4. Conscious and unconscious communications. 5. Creativity (literary, artistic, etc.) – Psychological concepts.

ISBN-13: 978-1-942431-12-1 (soft cover)

Front Cover Art Credit: Noyes Capehart: *Gray Day*, 1995, Watercolor, 9" x 12" (used with permission)

Book design, editing, and book cover - by MindMendMedia, Inc. @ MindMendMedia.com

TABLE OF CONTENTS

Publisher's Foreword (xiii)

Acknowledgements (xv)

Introduction (xvii)

The Author as Subject

Father and Mother (3)
Three Mothers, Plus One (4)
Attila, Fencer, Jew (9)
Beyond Twenty (11)
My Berlin (13)
My Mother's Bed (17)
Our Harmonium (19)
Life Sounds (22)
Two White Summer Suits (23)
A Different Story (25)
Howard and Peter (26)

For the Good Times

Little Yellow Flowers (28)
Snow in Hessen (30)
Borrowed View (31)
Coming Fall (32)
The View from the Ninth Floor (33)
Classic Bavaria (35)

It Can Get Worse

Never Without IT (39)
Of the Same Past (41)
My Holocaust (43)
Back Into the Future (45)
Our Dead are with Us Forever (47)
The Last Flight (49)

Franz Herda, American-German (53)
Am Stammtisch (55)
Entartete Kunst: Munich, July 1937 (57)
Toward the End, April 1945 (61)

Prescience

Tuesday Morning (65)
23rd and Park; 9 AM Saturday (67)
Stranger/s (69)
O' Christmas Tree (73)
The Other Browning of America (77)
Stormy Consequences. America 2015 (79)
Another Time Today (81)
The Sycophant (83)
Slogan-Makers (85)
Glorious Nation/s (87)
Authoritarians on the Rise (89)
A Pig's Beautiful Body (91)
Refugees/ *Flüchtlinge/ Profughi* (93)
History Should Teach Us Differently (95)
Bedtime Stories (96)
Don't Forget (98)
Adam and Eve (101)
After Us (103)

Conclusion (105)

Notes (107)

ACKNOWLEDGEMENTS

PUBLISHER'S FOREWORD

The dark thought, the shame, the malice.
Meet them at the door laughing and invite them in.
Be grateful for whatever comes.
Because each has been sent
as a guide from beyond. (Rumi, *The Guest House*)

MindMend Publishing is delighted to present to the world this book of existential poetry that cannot leave anyone indifferent. Dr. Peter Petschauer, originally a historian who became a poet psychohistorian, communicates with the reader freely, using original poetry, without clichés and pomposity. As a true historian, he records objective facts of life and his own life experiences, while examining openly the state of his being (rather than doing), as well as his feelings – about his past and present, and even the future.

Dr. Petschauer openly invites us to his "here-and-now," even if it makes him sad and vulnerable. He talks about his (very personal) past; his father who – he thought – was a hero, but ended up being a "Nazi, having lost … his world"; and his mother who – he thought – was "absent," but who was perfectly alive, but "lost in her own Middle Ages…" The author tells us a story of the world's affairs through the eyes of the person born in Berlin, a place that brings him pride and sorrow at the same time; a person who speaks the language of Goethe, Kant, Brahms, and … Hitler; a person who had four mothers, not just one; and lots of memories about lots of people and places; and memories permeated with love, grief, and human relationships – very much like in Proust's "madeleine moments."

Reading this volume will leave you with an appreciation of history not being a constellation of facts, but rather a living, breathing, and almost a synesthetic "thing" that reflects the very actual and factual life of the world – through the eyes of the beholder. This volume illustrates how each of us brings our own story to "what happened" and our own interpretations of the same events, and our own alliances, and connections, often unexpected.

History comes alive in this volume of *Hopes and Fears*, and we are grateful to Dr. Petschauer for sharing with us his authentic enthusiasm for life "as is," and his unending love to humanity.

Enjoy!

On behalf of MindMend Publishing,
Dr. Inna Rozentsvit

ACKNOWLEDGEMENTS

It is true that we are nothing without those around us – our family, members of our households, friends, acquaintances, companions, colleagues, and individuals with whom we happen to interact.

The latter sometimes leave a profound impression. I am thinking of an overly active three-year old Syrian girl in Erbach, Germany, whom I met during the winter of 2017. Joyful and enthusiastic, she kept running onto a judo competition mat where other children were going through their supervised routines. When her mother, somewhat frustrated, attempted to stop her, the child loudly accused the mother, "You don't like me anymore!" The mother replied soothingly, "Of course I love you. But don't interfere with the other children." All of this in German, the language they had learned recently. This moment resonated with me because the girl (mis)behaved like any other child would, in this situation; and her mother endeavored in age-old fashion, just like any other mother would there and in Syria, from which they had escaped; she continued to love and teach, but now in their new environment and with their new language.

First, I would like to acknowledge my friend and colleague Howard Stein. Over the course of a decade, Dr. Stein unstintingly encouraged my poetry writing. He offered feedback on many of my attempts, and most recently introduced me to Dr. Inna Rozentsvit, publisher and editor-in-chief of the ORI Academic Press and MindMend Publishing. Being embraced by a competent and caring editor is a true gift; and Inna is such a person. Howard and I, as reflected in the poem entitled "Howard and Peter," originated in very different backgrounds, but we are brothers at heart.

David Beisel was the first to see in me the potential for publishing poetry; he included some of my poems in *Wounded Centuries: A Selection of Poems* (NJ: Circumstantial Productions and Grolier Poetry Book Store, 2016).

If Stein and Beisel supported me in one way, Ed Pilkington pushed me to move beyond stolid history writing and to attempt instead more free-flowing texts. He encouraged a text from which persons other than academics could readily gain insights. The first play is to his credit. Noyes Capehart urged me to attempt a novel; once more emerged a venture beyond the traditional and an effort to leave behind the abuses of the 20th century. In the meantime, Drs. David Beisel and Paul Elovitz have been with me for decades in attempts to link history and psychology. Paul Elovitz in particular has pushed and pulled me to move beyond "classical" history. Some have called my poetry psychohistorical.

The credit for digging up and confronting over and over my family's and my own past goes to Dr. Zohara Boyd. We explored our different backgrounds in many presentations in elementary, high schools, colleges, and universities; she – as the child hidden in plain sight in Warsaw during WWII, and I – as the son of an SS lieutenant. Boyd and I began our relationship as colleagues at Appalachian State University, and we have since become a unique pair of friends.

Dr. Peter Lange reintroduced me to Berlin, the beautiful and energetic city on the Spree, in which I was born. Several years ago, he and I cooperated on research related to life of the German-American conductor Hans Schwieger. Lange's (2015) *Ein amerikanischer Europäer: Die zwei Leben des Dirigenten Hans Schwieger* (*An American European; the Two Lives of the Conductor Hans Schwieger*) has been a success. His astute journalist's eye opened for my wife Joni and me many of the sites significant in the 1930s and 1940s, and introduced us to exhibitions featuring important topics and reinterpretations.

Let me also mention the fellow poets Merle Molofsky and Irene Javors; Amy Hudnall, a student and now inspiring faculty member at Appalachian; and Lillian Nave, another successful colleague at the same institution. Without these people, the word *colleague* would have become meaningless. Each in her own way, they allowed me to reach beyond what university teaching and research would ordinarily have offered me.

Finally, I want to acknowledge the other women in my life! My wife Joni, without whom I would have been lost to love; my daughter Melanie who reminded me that her daughter does not yet appreciate depressing poems; and of course, my granddaughter who embodies any remaining hope for the future.

INTRODUCTION

In graduate school decades ago, I first discovered the Soviet Union's vast array of concentration and labor camps, and then – the National Socialist's mayhem of imprisonment and murder. These discoveries undermined the deep-seated optimism with which I had approached life since childhood. I realized soon enough that I had to recover this positive outlook without ignoring these horrors. Nevertheless, the cruelty of dictatorships, and my father's service in one of them, continued to undermine my optimism about others and about myself. And for decades, I hoped to work myself through the recognition and impact of the abuses, and I spoke and wrote about what I had learned. How could they? Is there anything to prevent such behavior in the future?

Poetry entered my life relatively late, and yet I experienced two breakthroughs almost effortlessly. First, I could express feelings precisely, while my academic historical work discouraged the deep emotional expression associated with some discoveries; and, to my dismay, I also realized that historical articles and books are read at best by a very small number of readers. Second, in spite of the past horrors with which I had become all too familiar, and my fears for the future, my inner optimism returned.

Most importantly, I accepted that my family, friends, and acquaintances in the Western World have lived in a long period of peace, in which we all, and the liberal arts, could thrive. While family and friends supported my successes and some of my failures, art has given Joni and me sustenance, and we are privileged to enjoy it in our home. Further, we have been able to support artists and museums.

Finally, music – from Vivaldi, Bach, Beethoven, Mahler, and Strauss, and all the way to New Orleans Jazz, Catharina Valente, the Beatles, and Pink Martini, to name a few, has provided me with infinite joy.

The poems in this volume are an expression of my love for people in my far and close circles, my optimism for life, hopes for the future, and the travails that have attempted to undermine both.

THE AUTHOR AS SUBJECT

Erich & Hildegard Dalmer Petschauer,
probably after their marriage during the winter of 1938 in Berlin.

FATHER AND MOTHER
Fall 2013
In Honor of Robert Gold Webb

Then, I was a child –
believing him a hero.
All too soon I was an adult –
searching for a father.
To my dismay I found a Nazi,
having lost … his world.

Then I was a child –
believing her absent.
All too soon I was an adult –
searching for a mother.
To my consternation
I found her in dementia and
lost in her own Middle Ages –
as Hildegard of Bingen.

Then I was a child –
with unknown parents.
Here I am now,
with an ordinary man and woman –
so distant and, yet,
with every thought and decision –
their concerns are mine.

Photos of Imperial officers,
and housewives.
Memories of teachers and doctors,
and housewives.

A splendid and troubled world,
so far removed, and yet much like mine,
made and unmade by realities of life.
Our world,
seemingly less destructive than theirs –
hardly more moral all the same.

THREE MOTHERS, PLUS ONE
Summer 2013
In Memory of Aloisia Petraider Clara,
Agnes Clara Obwexer, Hildegard Dalmer Petschauer,
and Emmie (Micky) Anders Petschauer

We all have one mother;
I had four.
All lived far away,
in Europe.

Two on farms, two in cities.
Each, in her own way,
caring and courageous,
beautiful and strong.

The farm women,
steady in their routine.
The city women,
resilient in their ingenuity.

As one misery stepped into the next –
that's how they survived.
World War One.
The Depression.
Mussolini and Hitler.
World War Two.

Fields churned, streets collapsed.
Villages and cities mourning their dead.
In graveyards, images of fallen soldiers
peered from columns and crosses.

And if that were not enough.
In our family,
mother, son, brother, sister –
gone forever.

Aloisia Petreider Clara,
Mutter Egarter.

Agnes (Neas) Clara Obwexer.

Hildegard Dalmer Petschauer.

Emmie (Micky) Anders Petschauer.

When will it end, dear Lord?
When will it end?

It did.

Sadly, one died too soon.
Three lived longer than most.
In peace.
Having learned to cope all too well…

*Photographs of my four mothers, presented above:

Aloisia Petreider Clara, Mutter Egarter. She took me in during WWII, and I accepted her as my role model.
Agnes (Neas) Clara Obwexer, Aloisia Petreider's daughter. We became mother and son.
Hildegard Dalmer Petschauer, my birth mother. All of her life we struggled to find each other.
Emmie (Micky) Anders Petschauer, my stepmother. She was my fourth mother; she adopted me and I adopted her. This photo was taken right after the WWII.

Attila Petschauer (1904-1943) was Hungarian Olympic champion fencer of Jewish heritage. He was tortured and died in a Nazi camp in Davidovka, Ukraine. His image may be found on the Internet.

ATTILA, FENCER, JEW
In Honor of Howard Stein
Spring 2014

I rediscovered you
not so long ago
on the Internet, no less.
Surely not by accident –
this other man with my family's name,
Hungarian and Jew, journalist and fencer!

Did my father know you?
Did you know my father?
Did either of you know Wilda?
The actor and writer –
our namesake in Prague?
A Jew as well, unlike my father,
who thought himself German –
from another province of Austria-Hungary;
the Empire that was home for you all.

Self-inflicted war destroyed
this collection of nations and ethnicities.
The victorious Allies freed you
from your imperial home –
they said you should fend for yourselves.
Instead, you fought each other,
having discovered your separate identities.

What were your parents thinking
when they named you Attila,
scourge of Europe so long ago?
Did they anticipate your fame
in the Olympics in 1928 and 1932?

Fencing was your métier.
You harvested medals –
became a national hero –
celebrated in press and radio.

But the Nazis* overran your country.
And like your namesake of Prague –
they tortured you to death
in a concentration camp.

Attila, how dare you disturb
my peace with your heritage?
A heritage that questions my own?
German and American –
son of a German from Slovenia.

Did my father know you?
Did my father know of you?
Did my father stay quiet
      to avoid guilt by association
            and death by camp?

*National Socialists

The slogan "WORK SETS FREE" was inserted into a number of gates to Nazi concentration camps. The shown banner appears above the gates to Auschwitz.

BEYOND TWENTY
*In Honor of Melanie Petschauer
Winter, 2013*

Twice it happened,
Three years apart;
women offering me a seat –
verifying the reality –
one cannot hide one's age
on public transportation.

Yet this inquiry
on a bus in Berlin
came as a surprise.
She was eighteen, maybe nineteen,
a veil covering her abundant hair.
She asked in excellent German:
"Would you like a seat?
I am getting off at the next stop."

"No, no," I offered in response,
"We are getting off as well."
But, I followed up:
"How do you know
that I turned older just last night?"

She saw right through me,
as if she knew
of the unexpected phone call
announcing the arrival of my daughter's child.

This news was far from my mind
on a bus in the city
in which I was born before the war –
and I had seen only once
since the Wall had come down.
On that snowy morning,
smiles and laughter all around –
not disapproving, not at all,

simply acknowledging:
another man had lived long enough
to be called
grandfather.

I had walked next to my youthful bride –
thinking:
I am eighteen –
surely not marching toward seventy-five.

A unique shot across the bow!

MY BERLIN
In Honor of Peter Lange
Winter 2015

From the first day of my life,
you were my home.
Not quite by accident,
Berlin, city on the Spree.

That moment, in that place –
interwoven with larger history:
Both never leaving me completely.
Returning me all too often
into the cauldron of passing times.

Florid speeches laden with bravado –
once filled the air with corroding lies.
Jackboots and martial songs –
jammed the streets with dread and joy.
And then, one horrific night –
Jewish shops and temples were destroyed.

That's when my parents conceived their child –
ignoring what else the Nazis had in mind.
But they should have seen the signs –
Hitler's agenda was known all too well.

One might assume today
that my name matched that of the first holder
of the Vatican's ancient throne.
But no,
the future king of Yugoslavia
happened to be in town.
He provided the inspiration –
as did the nickname
my father carried throughout his life.

The artists, the gays, and the Jews –
they loved the city so.
From around the world they came –
they energized the nation's thriving center;
a shining example to a vibrant world.

To the Nazis though,
these others were degenerates
to be harassed, denied, and murdered.
Not much question then what they were about.

Father and mother recognized the dictator's perversion
too late to make amends.
Their son was already born
to live with the consequences of their naiveté.

With the "Thousand-Year-Empire" up in flames –
the *Führer* killed himself deep underground –
bunkered-in like a cornered rat.
A nasty stench spread across the city.
Fat flies took over from the troops,
feasted greedily on trash piles and buried corpses.
On boulevards made for parades –
bikers replaced the elite's black cars.

THE AUTHOR AS SUBJECT

Barefoot children clambered over jumbled
                               bricks and stones –
disheveled women cleared mountains of debris.

Split in four,
the city seemed at its end.
A new dictatorship took hold in its East.
Only Allied airlifts saved the rest.

Toward the end of that other regime,
border policemen asked me into their quarter.
Vodka they thought would have me reveal –
the truth about my imperialist associations.
"How could it be," they asked,
"your German is so good?"
"Believe it or not,
I was born right here in the Charité."

When the city united again,
these men disappeared.
And others returned –
the young, the energetic, and the creative –
Germans, Poles, Jews, Italians,
and others from far away.

Surely in this lifetime,
the excesses of two dictatorships suffice.

*The author took the photograph of the Reichstag in Berlin on December 10, 2010.

The photograph was taken by the author in May 2015.

THE AUTHOR AS SUBJECT

MY MOTHER'S BED
In Honor of Karen Abrams
Summer 2016

My mother's bed –
we did not take it.
We left it behind in the house in Charleston
that had become our home.
The humble place spoke to us long ago –
we cared for it with deep emotion and attention.

We knew every part of this place –
the colors of the paint,
the Caribbean grass on the steps,
and the glass light fixture over the dining table –
we bought down the street from a restoration store.

The house had become our home
away from home.
My mother's bed was part of its décor.
It stood unobtrusively in the dining room.
We loved the thought of having it nearby.

To see the place abused!
Trash piled high,
dust on dust,
black dog hair on the green couch.

She slept in the bed in Rhineland's Düsseldorf.
We brought it back to the U.S.
It reminded us of her.
The innards of the trundle she covered
with a damask curtain, and
affixed along its upper edge
with tiny nails an embroidered border.
It fit her person and her style.
We left it.
Too much heartache to take it along!

The new owners had abused the house –
they trashed my mother's memory.
They covered soft wood with their daily lives
and obscured the essence of this home.

This home –
our home,
no more than a house again –
the bed no more than a trundle.

OUR HARMONIUM
*In Honor of Emma Obwexer Frener
and in Memory of her Uncle Albert Clara
Winter 2016*

    Your soft notes filled the air again,
    before Christmas –
    some years ago.
    Stille Nacht, Heilige Nacht.
    You offered background to a play
    about poet and composer.

    For decades,
    you suffered silently in our barn –
    abandoned and abused.

You kept quiet about the cold and the heat,
the dust and the chickens.
One of your keys had frozen,
a pedal had come loose.

A younger family member thought of you –
and now you rang out once more.
Repaired and restored,
you helped recreate the famous story.

I did not recognize you sitting down below.
You!
The first memory of my earliest years.
Then, many decades ago,
you stood in the corner of the living room,
the *Stube* of our Dolomite farm.
You were a welcome gift from Agnes,
the teacher,
to Albert,
her nephew and aspiring organist.

My father played you then.
I see him still:
dark hair,
white shirt,
suspenders across the back,
a cigarette just relit.

Surrounded by the nephew and his sisters –
you provided background
for glorious mountain songs.
Over the tattered notes on your stand,
player and singers looked out
on the narrow path to the church.

Humble harmonium!
You up there on the stage!

Surrounded by actors recreating moments of 1818.
Did you recall those summer moments of '42?

Then, when your varnish was still fresh –
your pedals gave sufficient air,
and every key hit its note?

Or did you thankfully forget the time after '45?
Then,
when Albert was brutally murdered in Yugoslavia,
and then, too, when the family moved you into the barn?

You were alive once more –
when Franz Xavier Gruber's representative played you
to accompany Joseph Mohr's famous composition.
Your varnish shone.
The two pedals offered air.
All keys played in tune.
Just long enough!
Before you were banished again.

*The photograph of Albert Clara was most likely taken by Foto Erich Planinschek (Brixen/Bressanone) in 1942/1943. The original photograph is in Emma Obwexer Frener's possession, and its reproduction is used with her permission.

LIFE SOUNDS
*In Honor of Sabrina Marchioro and Walter Frenzel
Spring 2016*

The clatter of three horses' hoofs –
below a window.
A small town in Bavaria.

The bells of a Baroque church.
In the mountains of Northern Italy.

The screeching of a streetcar on the corner –
in the middle of the night.
A city in the Rhineland.

The scratching of a mouse –
in a garbage can.
The house on Grand Boulevard.

The voices of colleagues –
in the department.
A university in the Appalachian Mountains.

The transparency of Antonio Vivaldi's violins –
as if played once more.
Venice right here now.

The clicking of a computer's keyboard –
in many places –
around the globe.

Falling asleep –
regular thumping of two hearts.

The soft breathing of my beloved partner –
in a shared bed. Reassurances of life.

THE AUTHOR AS SUBJECT

TWO WHITE SUMMER SUITS
*In Memory of Josef Roth
Late Spring 2016*

A cousin gave him a summer suit.
That was in June of 1941.
A white summer suit in Warsaw's infamous ghetto!
Josef rejoiced in a note to his daughter:
What a wonderful gift!
Yet he realized:
It will not suffice in Poland's brutal winters.
He needed underwear and sweaters,
and items to trade.
Trading food and clothing
assured starving and freezing inhabitants –
a few more days of survival.

Far away in Manhattan,
his daughter seemed not to understand,
too far removed to comprehend
the implications of his joy and dilemma, and requests.
In his two years in the ghetto,
he received one package from NYC.
Did the guards steal the rest?

The notes from one of Eastern Europe's
                                      worst calamities
clawed themselves out of an attic –
in a small town in New Jersey in the 1990s.
Again and again,
the granddaughter asked herself:
Was her mother, his daughter, that unaware?
How could she ignore her father's pleas?
She must have known about this miserable place.

She did not.
He withheld the truth in pleasant phrases:
"Otherwise we are fine."
"Do not worry about us."
"Mother sends her greetings."

Descendants learned the cruel truth
less than a decade later:
The godforsaken place in the midst of Poland's capital
was their family members' only temporary abode.
But by then it was too late –
they had long since perished in Treblinka.

Seeing his problem as winter and survival,
Josef reported about his suit, unaware of his eventual fate.

The white suit's message reverberates in my mind
like one of Mozart's melodies.

Totally unrelated –
nearly two decades after Josef's murder –
an uncle in New Jersey offered me a barely worn
                                        white summer suit,
a welcome gift upon my arrival in the U.S.
He wore it on festive occasions and in Vegas.
A colorful tie completed the ensemble.

I strutted down Manhattan's Fifth Avenue
in the summer heat –
proud and clueless of the passé style.
As unaware as Josef was of his surroundings' implications,
I was of mine.
Except that his journey ended in an untimely death –
mine in a better life.

A DIFFERENT STORY
In Honor of all Veterans
Fall 2017

Sometimes
in a wheelchair in an airport,
I wish front-line duty had been in my past.

Some fellow travelers approve with a smile,
others avert their gaze –
not wanting to face their own future frailty.
Some believe –
ski poles and neck brace, no more than fake.

Except for these aids,
the injuries are invisible.
I want to tell the observers,
the empathizers and the doubters:
Inattention with a lawnmower took the right foot's toe –
not a land mine's dirty deed in some far away front,
like Afghanistan or Syria.
I would like to yell out as well:
My hands hurt not because of too much typing –
it was the heat of machine gun barrels
held in long-since forgotten desert wars.
My head braced and held high –
not because of too much leaning over typewriters
                                      and iPads,
but from a misplaced shrapnel.

How reassuring it would be to scream out loudly,
not silently:
I am a hero,
I fought for you,
I gave my body so you could be free.

HOWARD AND PETER
Late Summer 2013

Friends, but not born that way.
Brothers, but not in a single mothers' womb.

Life threw us together --
for reasons unknown.
Minds and souls singing with each other,
like birds of the same feather.

Physically ever so distant –
rare the moments next to each other.
Conversations ebb and flow,
as we share a rare meal together.

Capacities far apart as well,
yet interests constantly interweaving.
Genius tolerating average,
average accepting genius.

The personal rarely interjected.
Your son with troubles I never knew –
loving, caring, one of you.
Decade after decade, my child rejecting,
refusing to find a common ground.

Hardships soften in friendship's womb.
Brothers,
        friends,
                and fathers.

FOR THE GOOD TIMES

LITTLE YELLOW FLOWERS
In Honor of Cindy Wallace and Allen Moseley
Spring 2014

Little yellow flowers,
harbingers of spring.
Just yesterday you waited
for your time deep under snow.

Like the sun –
you give a hint
of the warmth to come.

Your petals so frail and gentle
like the sun of spring –
not yet matured
to oppressive summer heat.

We admire your courage,
little flowers.
Surely you know
how easily you can succumb
to another snow.

FOR THE GOOD TIMES

Somewhat like a baby,
cooing at the attention of her mother –
unaware of the difficult road ahead.

You are like peace
after seeming eons of misery and cold.
Unaware that it too can be crushed
once more by men and women
who did so before.

Cold snow,
please don't crush our petals;
brutal men and women,
please don't abuse our bodies.

Was it not enough
that we survived your last assault?
Is it not enough
that we stand brightly still
to honor the better part of us all?

*The photograph was taken by the author in the garden of the family's former home in Boone in the spring of 2016.

SNOW IN HESSEN
*In Honor of Fenja Petschauer
February 2018*

Wet snow bending green branches –
white wool for a colder day.

Strong wind gusts lifting blankets –
heavy loads falling to the ground.

Branch after branch –
snapping back into place.

BORROWED VIEW
*In Memory of Matsuo Basho
Spring 2015*

Frail branches hold
untold fluffy balls
of white and pink.
Millions of petals –
clustered just above.

Spring is here.
Inspired fleeting moments.

Barely kissed
by the warming sun.
Gentle breezes assist
tiny flakes to the ground.

The flowering glory ends.
Green leaves emerge.
Winter has departed.

*Photograph was taken by Joni Petschauer, the author's wife, in Washington DC in the spring of 2015.

COMING FALL
Fall 2017

Cool breezes –
anticipate cooler weather –
wipe away summer's sweat.

Spent leaves –
drift to the ground --
crumble on the rim of the path.

Glistening rays –
intensify spots of green –
illuminate a tree's naked trunk.

Two bucks and a doe –
ears forward –
momentarily attentive to our presence.

Observing ourselves as intruders –
silent in this spectacle.

*Photograph taken by the author at Bass Lake, Blowing Rock, NC, in the fall of 2017.

THE VIEW FROM THE NINTH FLOOR
In Honor of Joni Petschauer
Winter 2017

Like broad rivers –
day in and day out.
Massive amounts of water,
flowing to and fro.
The ocean visible in the distance.

They inundate and relinquish the island further down.
Multitudes of houses guard the rest of the shore.
Hundreds of boats,
rarely taken out to sea, anchored,
as if abandoned.

A man in his boat –
two dogs looking out over the keel,
anticipating landing on the island,
jumping off even before he lands.
They are on their daily toilet run –
no need to worry here about their waste;
the tide will carry it away.

A pelican swooping down –
breaking the glistening surface,
having discovered fish below.
Blackbirds settling on sailboat masts –
watching the scenery and looking for enemies,
releasing their droppings on decks below.
Two seagulls chasing one another,
as if happy to fly in the sun –
oblivious to the observer
on the balcony.

*Photograph taken by the author in November of 2017.

FOR THE GOOD TIMES

CLASSIC BAVARIA
In Honor of Stefan Foag
Summer 2014

The stations are close together,
        the names come loud and clear:
Traunstein, Bergen, Übersee,
        Bernau, Prien, Bad Endorf.
Small towns along Lake Chiem –
        heartland of Bavaria.

School boys and girls –
        hopping on and off.
Wild conversations –
        talking, not listening.
Tourists and hikers –
        faces content.
Glorious sights rediscovered –
        familiar heights climbed anew.
Travelers on the way to the big cities –
        ignoring all but the screens of their phones.
Rosenheim and Munich not far off.

Lake Chiem barely hidden behind trees and houses,
glistening in the sun.

Ducks flying by,
looking for dinner.
People looking up from their coffee –
cake sure to follow soon.

*Photograph taken by the author of Lake Chiem in early winter 2016.

IT CAN GET WORSE

Erich Petschauer, in the middle of the photo, arms crossed, next to an Italian officer. Second on the left is his aide Herrmann Pitscheider (he called himself *Lehrbub*, or apprentice). As of 2018, he still lived in Brixen/Bressanone).

The photograph was most likely taken on the *Domplatz/Piazza Duomo* in the spring of 1941.

NEVER WITHOUT IT
In Memory of Dr. Erich Petschauer
Fall 2017

Whatever that IT might be –
We're never beyond IT.
Like the eternal flame,
IT burns forever.

We go to bed,
We get up,
We put breakfast on the table,
We send the kids to school,
We drive to work,
We listen to our music,
We read the news,
We write about new themes,
We leave the past behind.

I thought –
I too had moved beyond IT –
the IT of my father's service in a
                    terrorist organization.
But then a colleague sent a black and white –
1941 stamped on the back.

In the main square of a small town in Italy –
a large mass of young and old
looking up.
In Sunday attire.

He stands there as well –
in the center of it all,
the Italian liaison next to him.
Unlike his colleague.
he was out of uniform –
simply sporting a Hitler mustache
and the NS party pin on the left lapel.

Hands crossed on his chest –
eyes fixed straight ahead,
listening yet observing.
Did he hear the speaker above?
Or see the pickpocket cutting
the wallet out of a man's pant pocket?
Right there, my father recounted later –
with dignitaries all around!
Or was he saying to himself:
What am I doing here?

There I was again –
at my father's side in the 1940s.
My colleague did not understand my consternation.
Don't forget, he wrote,
he was doing a good job.

Yes indeed,
a good job with the SS!

OF THE SAME PAST
In Memory of the Survivors
Winter and Spring 2015

The three arrived within days of each other.
Two had Auschwitz numbers on their arms,
one had the SS blood-type indicator under his.
The three were members of a common past.
Did they know each other at the peak of their years?

The home for older persons took them in;
no one asked about their past.
"Insurance coverage? Yes? Or No?"
That's what interested the staff.

No personal or family experience
allowed them to see beyond
their patients' immediate needs.
Their awareness of history did not include
that other time,
even as its representatives
shuffled through their door.

That time of fitting uniforms and shiny boots –
and glorious battles fought far away.
That misery of cruel isolation and denigration –
and personal battles to survive.

That other time was as if forgotten –
thick fog covering their youth.
Poor health had chased them out of seclusion –
into public rooms to exist indefinitely.

Dementia's power was not complete.
A survivor howled one day.

Not to be consoled –
she screamed for several more.

She was Russian-born,
the nurse pulling the fog from her mind.
The young woman's face evoked a deeply
                                            buried
                                                memory:
The old woman saw clearly again –
a guard dragging her to selection.

Awareness had opened the door to the past –
the staff knew what to do.
The order was short and clear:
"Keep them apart –
in the cafeteria and outside."

Just one more recognition,
unfurling carefully orchestrated routines.

MY HOLOCAUST
In Honor of Amy Hudnall
Spring 2014

The cards and letters of a Polish Jew
                              found me first.
He had arrived in the Warsaw Ghetto.
In beautiful German script
he implored his relations in America.
In hopefulness and despair,
he pleaded for them to hear his cries.
His family could not read what he wrote –
better than his guards.

These signals from the past –
decades later re-awakened an ugly reality
in an attic in New Jersey.
So far removed in space and time
re-arose the quest to understand,
the fate of an uncle in wartime Poland.

He dreaded the onset of winter –
when he found a white summer suit.
Salvation seemed at hand –
but winter was not the problem.
America did not want more educated Jews.
Treblinka became his destination next July.

The child from Warsaw and I found each other next.
As college professor and colleague,
she became my friend.
Her parents, his sister and she
moved from house to house, cellar to cellar.
In plain sight as Poles and in constant fear –
never knowing when it all would end.

Two passing German soldiers shot her dad.
He lived with a scar on his back to recall the attack.

The stain returned in her dreams –
white shirts bleeding time after time.
She never could forget.

Bombs rained down on their basement –
destruction, dust, and death all around.
Her side stood, the other fell.
The others died –
every man, woman, and child.
Her group survived.
God of Jews and Christians,
what was the fairness in that?

I found him last,
the great Jew and German literary critic.
They sent him back to Poland in 1939 –
his studies in Berlin never to resume.
As secretary of the *Judenrat,*
he practiced German and typing instead.
They found no one else for the job.

His notes became the record
for that infamous day in July –
when SS troops announced the Ghetto's dissolution.
The shot next door took him from his typist's chore –
his boss had killed himself in despair.

He stumbled with his wife across a field of ruins.
They thought better to die with bullets in their backs
than a gas filled chamber.
No shots rang out for them that day.

The first was Josef Roth,
the second is Zohara Mushinsky Boyd,
and the third was Marcel Reich-Ranicki.

BACK INTO THE FUTURE
In Honor of Zohara Boyd
Spring and Summer 2015

They keep coming back –
the outrageous memories of the past.
They torture my dreams –
turn miserable my days.

Irresistibly they remain with me –
the men and women in uniform –
striped, tattered, and stained.
The children, the aged and infirm as well –
on their way to chambers of death.
Trains brought them to camps in Europe –
trucks rolled them to forests in Siberia.

Once more, they walk –
naked and harangued
to a shower that sprays gas,
not water.

In a field far to the East –
others stand naked and ashamed,
waiting for a bullet.
And they come to me again –
men, women, and children,
citizens of Germany, Austria, Poland, Russia,
and France.

Doctors, painters, carpenters, plumbers,
                                      and their wives.
Teachers, preachers, professors, rabbis,
                                      and their wives.
Composers, tailors, musicians, lawyers,
                                      and their wives.
With certainty they knew
the Gestapo would spare them:
They had worked for the common good.

Trustingly they thought
the NKVD would not knock on their door:
they had toiled incessantly for Party and country.

Why let into dreams and awareness
long-ago tales of woe?
Why re-run horrors of generations ago?
Don't we have our own?

Behind their black masks,
killers smirk at lessons from the past:
Do not kill, torture, and abuse.
Instead –
they enjoy their endless spree
of bloodshed, destruction, and depravity.

It is the double-edged sword of the past:
Religion perverted.
   Traditions distorted.
      Laws corrupted.
         Humanity abandoned.

OUR DEAD ARE WITH US FOREVER
In Honor of David Beisel
Spring 2014

They inhabit my dreams –
with murderous instructions and terrified screams.
They frighten my nights
and hollow out my days –
the people killed in the '30s and '40s.

They lie buried in Poland, Germany, and Austria –
and from there to the deepest forests of Siberia.
They are quiet only at work –
when the sun shines on my life.
At night, when the world is still,
they shake off ashes for their visit.

Germans killed communists,
           socialists, Gypsies, and Jews.
Russians killed communists,
              farmers, soldiers, and Jews.
Germany's number one enemies were
                  Jews and Germans.
Russia's number one enemies were Russians.

Jews and Germans murdered –
understood to be the perpetrators' target.
Knowing themselves different –
they would surely be marked for death.
Russians killed understood –
the murderers had marked them by mistake.
If only Stalin knew, they would remain alive.
Stalin knew.
Millions went to their deaths.
Most without a trial –
without proper food and clothing –
alone and in groups.

They died in deep forests, in filthy trains,
                              in open fields, in hot labs,
to impossible work as they marched in the snow.

Families forever scarred –
their own murdered by shots they never heard –
suffocated in chambers they never entered.
Not understanding why their societies
                              betrayed their own –
not knowing the resting place of their beloved.

Germans avoided their crimes until the '60s –
shocked by projections of their inner evil
                                  onto the Other,
the gay, the Gypsy, the Jew, the German, the Pole…

Russians avoided their crimes until the 2000s –
suppressing the evil deeds on their own.
With most perpetrators and victims gone –
their misery stays without resolution.

THE LAST FLIGHT
In Memory of Raymond Zisk
Spring 2014

Confident in themselves and their cause –
they knew their missions justified.
They laughed, kidded, played cards –
not concerned about dangers in the sky,
nor the harvest of their bombs.

The young men flew unhampered;
the German air force had disappeared.
Daily they demolished further north –
industries, bridges, churches, houses,
and human beings.

The planes were their friends:
Guns threatened from every opening –
and fighters hovered nearby.

Squadrons – they were called –
waves of planes droning in the sky –
bursting ears and rattling windows.
Rumbling turning louder –
resolving in explosions and destruction.

The men of the FLAK responded with their cannon.
Confident of their mission,
few realizing its fundamental flaw.
They created black puffs of exploding munitions –
tiny clouds high up in the sky.

The detonations rocked the fliers –
"Damn Krauts! Give it up!"
A missive passing beneath,
like a bird in pursuit of prey.
Said a veteran later:
"Nearly shit in my pants that day."

On the last day of February '45 –
an 88 found its mark.
Twelve Americans did not survive the war –
Jews, English, Poles --
all Americans.

The fiery detonation lingers seven decades later –
like the images of two pieces tumbling down.
A parachute helped one gunner out –
he lived a night before he died.
The other left without a head
and was lost in the snow.

A gentle meadow received the fuselage –
snow kept it unexploded –
an arm and hand dangling from a window –
leaving ten men in a final good bye.

No doubt, dictatorships needed eradication –
under their leaders' yoke –
the villagers lived in destitution.

On that bitter day in February –
twelve Americans joined these men and women –
ordinary human beings
in desperation taking provisions and possessions.

In a moment of true humanity
                            and without discussion,
the men who suffered dictatorships
                            and liberating bombs
dug a temporary resting place
                            for the foreign fighters.

They found their resting place later
in far-away America.
High up in the mountains
stands today a cross in honor of their sacrifice.

*Photograph taken by the author in the spring of 2015.

Franz Herda
Photograph from *Das Traunsteiner Tagblatt*
(*Vintage 2015*, #48; 11/28/2015).

IT CAN GET WORSE

FRANZ HERDA, AMERICAN-GERMAN
Winter 2015

Franz Herda,
a man one can admire:
American and German alike –
painter and opponent of the NS regime.

Friedrich Percyval Reck-Malleczewen,
odd noble opponent of the regime,
called him friend.
Albertine Gimpel,
the Jewess he hid from the Gestapo,
called him husband.

Born in Brooklyn to German-Americans –
Bavaria drew him to study art.
He remained to observe the regime:
Before he knew the complexity of mean.
The U.S. passport kept him free –
allowed him to become engaged.

In Munich from SA* hoodlums,
he saved a woman and a man:
A blond German and a starred Jew.
Did the man land in Dachau,
or worse,
like his friend?

Denounced twice by his publisher –
Reck-Malleczewen found there his death in 1945.

Herda could save his wife in Bavaria –
but post-war hopes were foiled in the U.S.
Even Einstein's support for naught –
portraits of him and others brought no success.

He lies buried with his wife,
in the place of his finest success –

in Bavaria ...
where he confronted the nastiest regime.

Zivilcourage they called it then:
Germany in the '30s and '40s.
Civil Courage they called it later:
the U.S.A. in the 50s.
To stand up to men
who scorn values that make us human.
Those who had others trample willingly
                                  on their fellows.
Civil courage:
We need it again today.
To face up to men spreading fear and hate.
Applying tactics of these other times –
cynically exploiting the weak and unprepared.

Two Josephs come to mind:
Goebbels and McCarthy.
Disseminators of half-truths and lies.
Relentless efforts to oppress foes and,
before long ... adulators.

*50 years after Franz Herda's death, Yad Vashem, the memorial in Jerusalem, Israel awarded him the honorary title "Righteous among the Nations" – for helping Jewish people during the rule of the Nazi party.
*SA. *Sturmabteilung* (Storm Detachment, or "Assault Division," or Brownshirts, one of Hitler's many quasi military units).

AM STAMMTISCH
In Honor of Marianne Saller
Winter 2015

After their morning beer,
most regulars had left.
As far back as anyone could tell,
men like them,
after Sunday mass
had taken their libation here --
their reward for surviving unscathed --
another service that reminded of their sins.

He hung there patiently –
listening to our chatter.
Speaking different dialects –
our group, too, being from the area.
Our conversation was not of the
                              earthshaking kind –
the weather and the food
were the main concerns.
The air was clean and the half-liter tasted cool.

Lunch at a *Stammtisch* in Bavaria.
The carved table held our meal –
as it had for generations.
Like the table,
the Nazareen Carpenter
had lost a few details and some color.
Eighty years ago –
the place filled with smoke.
Men pounded fists on darkened wood.
Their mouths spouted hostile phrases.
Hatred rang through the place.

The figure on the cross –
rusty nails in extremities –
a deep wound on the right.
Blood running down his arms and his side.

Lungs filled with smoke,
he heard them shout:
Hitler is winning the election.
Protestants and Jews,
finally will disappear from our sight.

The young Jew on the cross –
the King of the Jews.
INRI the Romans had written.
These men left him alone.
He could have told them –
had they heard.
The hate that murdered him would soon
kill half of them.

*Jesus in Erlstätt. Photograph taken by the author during the winter of 2019.

ENTARTETE KUNST:
Munich, July 1937
In Honor of Noyes Capehart
Summer and Fall 2015

Thousands came and admired –
six hundred works of art.
It is degenerate –
the Nazis had declared.
Thousands of works they had assembled,
but the ***cognoscenti*** reserved their
                                      pronounced disdain
for this small group.
And they hung it to distraction.

They stood around, feet spread wide –
brown uniforms and black boots.
Most ignored the haunting voices crying out –
few perceived the conscience of Germany.
Hitler attended, smirked and left.
Jews, he muttered, for most to hear.

A thousand others studied and discussed
dismembered limbs –
gas in crumbling trenches –
old men leering at prostitutes –
cigarettes dangling from women's mouths.

This art, they said,
speaks to me.
I understand this new approach.
Here are the horrors of World War One.
These are the questions of our tumultuous times.

Does it matter who created this art?
Jew or German?
Gay or straight?
Woman or man?
These are the realities of our days.

Millions stayed away from this July aberration –
they ignored the latest trend.
They overlooked the horrors of the past
and the NS present –
portrayed so succinctly in Munich's show.

Tradition was their home.
Just a bunch of urbanites.
Jews no less!
And gays for sure!
No discussions needed
about aberrations of this century.

Their Christ hung stretched and bleeding –
he had since the erection of their church.
This cruelty was stylized and familiar.
His tortured figure avoided confrontation –
with the barbarity of Ancient Rome
or their modern world.

They did not recognize the nakedness of Christ.
Only deep inside reverberated
the agony he bore for them.
Some NS ideologues shrewdly discerned –
these naive folks' desire
to view beauty of another kind.
Their younger brothers and sisters –
in the nude.
Not hanging, not tortured, not mutilated.
On paper and in marble.
Distant in a way –
close in another –
bloodless.

Clean shaven, sleek and slender –
female bodies –
so feminine.

Clean shaven, sinewy and muscular –
male bodies –
ever so masculine.
No torture here,
Just allure, serenity, and lies.

Adolf Hitler at the exhibit of *Entartete Kunst* (Degenerate Art),
July 19, 1937

* "Entartete Kunst" – "degenerate art," a term given by Nazis to modern art. Their disdain for modern art does not mean that all of it was particularly good and/or valuable. Neither does the Nazis' embrace of "traditional" art mean that all of it was poor or invaluable.

German soldiers; location unknown.
Photo is from the Internet stock photos.

TOWARD THE END, APRIL 1945

In Memory of Micky Petschauer
Spring 2015

They dangled from the rafters –
a lieutenant and a captain.
Belts held them off the floor –
four eyes staring nowhere.

My God!
Oh my God!

An overturned cot –
a polished boot on the ground –
a wet spot spread on a pair of pants –
a tongue dangling from a mouth.
How many more? – she asked.
No others today, he said.
Three yesterday.
There'll be more tomorrow.

We have come for food –
she fumbled for her words.

We have no food today,
the enemy blew up the truck on its way.
Oh no, not again.

You hang there so grizzly,
telling us part of your tale.

Young warriors:
Why, tell us, why?
What did you hear?
What did you see?
What did you do?
Was it despair or disillusion?
Or both –
that brought you to this end?

Did you predict more hangings tomorrow?
Don't know, he said,
Don't know!
Maybe we'll get some food tomorrow?
Don't know, he said.
Maybe, maybe not!

It's not over yet.

PRESCIENCE

This photograph of Washington Square taken by the author at the outset of June 2016.

TUESDAY MORNING
*In Honor of Nancy and Mark Tafeen
June 9, 2014*

The joy of emerging –
from one's building.
Bright sun shining –
dark glasses on one's nose.
Cool breezes ruffling one's hair –
wind tugging at the coat.

And right there –
a black woman walking with
three white children –
talking in staccato every step of the way.
Off to school, for sure.

A youngish man –
half-way up the street –
still dressing;
nice shirt, pink, a bit wrinkled.
Off to an interview.
Hey, what're staring at, old man?
Nothing really, nothing!

And then,
there she was, as I knew she would –
the goddess, not of my dreams –
but glorious, tall, fashionable all the same.
No phone in her ear.

Time stood still, for a second.
As quickly as she had appeared –
she disappeared around the corner.

The smell of coffee –
A conversation in Spanish –

a man doing exercises right there
on the sidewalk.

Hey, man, what's up?
Nothing really, nothing.

After all,
this is mid-town Manhattan –
on a Tuesday morning.

PRESCIENCE

23RD and PARK
9 AM SATURDAY
Summer 2016

Manhattan morning!
Everyone in a hurry.
Looking into my eyes,
not seeing them,
not seeing me.
Avoiding genuine contact –
staring into nothingness.
Cells in every hand.
Favorite tunes feeding eager ears.

"You read this T-shirt.
That is enough interpersonal
                            connection for the day."
Male and female runners –
as if preparing for the Olympics.
A mid-aged woman, a mother maybe,
sprinting behind a high-end baby carriage.
Sportswear from the finest NY boutique.

Two Chinese girls in short shorts –
grandmothers surely having complained:
What are you thinking?
What?
Thinking?
Short shorts?
Really!

The stone-faced couple --
an apartment fight visible in the street.
Hands surely held another Saturday morning.

An older woman,
hat askew,
looking for a humble breakfast.
Only wheat muffins?

Neither buckwheat nor spelt?
What happened to the other grains?
No explanation from behind the counter.

A man leaning against a doorframe,
the cigarette between index and middle fingers,
the hand never reaching his mouth;
he avoided inhaling the poisonous smoke.
A sad morning again!

A female cop pasting tickets on cars –
they stood on the wrong side of the street.
A city worker taking half an hour –
to refurbish a garbage can.

The latest skyscraper on 23rd –
watching the city below from the 50th floor.

STRANGER/S
To Honor NYC Homeless
August 2013

As the door opened,
she stood –
flip flops, shortest shorts, disheveled hair –
a child over her shoulder;

she was sound asleep,
as children are wont to be –
in the middle of the night.

Who are you?
Who invited you here?
Where is your luggage?

At a friend's apartment!
Didn't you get the message,
I called ahead.
Someone answered the phone:
It's OK, he said,
to come over late.

It was just past twelve –
when she stood in our elevator door.
My image of the Virgin and the Child
dissolved in the suspicion of her purpose.

A stranger.
Who are you?

I have permission to be here –
they said in the office that I have permission!

Did they tell you not bring a child?
This place is for adults only.

They did not ask.
I assumed I could; we are still on vacation.

You assumed?

My girl, she is so tired.
I need to put her down.
She is heavy.
She needs to sleep.

Let's lay her on a bunk –
She can sleep there and be safe.

A mother and her child after all.

Do you have family around here?

Yes, downtown,
in the Village.
But I am not welcome there.
You know, well,
I left my husband years ago.

Surely your daughter has a grandmother there?

She does, but the woman has rejected me.

Have you gone to see her?
Talked with her?

No, not really.
No!
We're distant now.

Strange, your daughter has a grandmother
and you avoid her closest kin?

She is not like my grandmother.
Stranger once more.
Where are you headed tomorrow?

Nowhere. I want to stay here.

PRESCIENCE

With your daughter?

With my daughter.

You know that's not possible.

Can't I stay here alone?

Better not stay without her – anywhere.
She loves you and she'll be alone.

Homeless, that's what you were –
I finally figured it out.
It was all around you --
that laden subway smell --
the one that ascends from its steely grates.

A good night's sleep,
A warm shower,
A clean child.
And a stranger forever.

*This conversation took place in Appalachian State University's NY Loft in August of 2013.

This photograph was taken by the author on Christmas Day in 2015 in the home of Martina and Hans Schölzhorn in South Tyrol/Alto Adige.

O' CHRISTMAS TREE
Late Winter 2014

Here I lie in the sun –
by the side of the road.
I am brown now –
with the full form of my body,
my needles, and my woodland smell.

Once, a long time ago,
I stood among my friends,
embedded comfortably in our world.
Barely ten years old,
with a strong center and solid limbs –
soft green needles covering my every inch –
healthy sap rushing through my veins.
That was me,
                then.

None of my friends was prettier than I.
When white fluff settled on me,
I felt cold and, yet,
white suited me even better than green.

Two-legged creatures came by one day –
jabbering as they went.
They were different than my friend, the rabbit –
he did not jabber;
he was not loud.

They looked at me –
jabbered some more and wound
                            a ribbon on my side.
As they walked away –
they placed ribbons on my friends.
Surely they are not as pretty as I!

I awoke from a fitful sleep;
the creatures had returned.

One of their little ones jumped around –
just like the rabbit,
except she too jabbered,
pointing this way and that.

With a start, the biggest creature roared.
Stepping toward me, it cut my trunk.
I ached and groaned,
but for the noise, it did not hear my cry:
"You are hurting me!"

It cut off my feet.

They wrapped me in a net,
like the spider spinning her slender thread.
This one though was coarse and cold –
not gentle like my spider's web.

"It's too tight, far too tight for me," I said –
it did not matter.

They took me from my friends –
they broke my heart.
I called out to them,
but I could not raise my voice.
When I tried to wave to them,
my limbs were bound.

Finally,
finally, the creatures took off the web
and gave me water.
Once more, they stood and jabbered:
"The best we ever had."

When the creatures left,
I saw my friends –
as if in a haze, far away.

They did not hear my cries of pain:

PRESCIENCE

"Please, please, take me back.
I will never think or say,
'You are not as pretty as I.'"

The creatures had another pain for me:
they wound heavy strings around –
everywhere they found a spot.
If my spider could have told them –
they would have known about stiff cords,
brittle limbs, and frail needles.

The next day, they brought me packages,
and jabbered about the bright lights on my limbs.
When they settled down,
they made bird-like noises, ugly
                                 screeching noises –
"Oh Tannenbaum."

How I miss our birds!

I felt it coming on.
My body weakened,
my sap dried up,
my limbs bent down.
The little creature noticed soon enough
and cried about my state.

No sooner had she spoken,
the big one picked me up and tossed me out –
left me in the cold –
no white fluff fell down to cover me.
I saw no friends and no friends saw me.

When he heard me cry –
he dragged me to the street, in the sun.

Once more, my friends were not far off –
the wind brought the sweet sound of their voices.

I had kept my needles and my shape.
Now a brownish stranger –
they were unaware of our common past.
And with my faded voice –
I could not tell them of my fate.

PRESCIENCE

THE OTHER BROWNING OF AMERICA
In Honor of Paul Elovitz
Summer 2013

They said, it won't happen here:
This is a democracy.

We told them that
it's happened before –
in a democracy.

They called us liberals;
saying it as if we were
socialists and communists.

We told them that it all happened before –
to our grandfathers in another democracy.

They told us:
We are doing it for your good –
streamlining things and saving money.

We told them:
You're stealing our votes,
our education and our wombs.

They said we're imagining things –
saying it as if –
we are fools and never-do-wells.

We told each other:
This happened before.
It is getting dangerous.

That's when they hauled us off to prison –
accusing us of being traitors.
Us, honorable citizens.

That's when we whispered to each other:
This happened before.

*In Germany,
not even a 100 years ago.*

Those living in the present,
not looking for before and after.
Fooled to their detriment.

This photograph was taken by the author near
Erlstätt, Germany, on December 13, 2015.

STORMY CONSEQUENCES.
AMERICA 2015
In Honor of Jay Wentworth
Fall 2015

The latest storm
arrived with alarming bursts,
pulsating –
like blood in our veins.

It came so suddenly –
without time to announce
its chilling and unrelenting cold.

Shivering, we learned soon enough
that this was the beginning
of another miserable time!

The storm's haste so dramatic,
its gusto so unabashed –
it tore leaves from branches --
chasing them like flocks of birds,
scattering them every which way.

The winds carved their own paths –
fierce, bitter, mean, unrelenting.
1933 falling into 2016 –
once more fall jumped into winter.

Banning books.
Tearing art from museums' walls.
Dismissing teachers.
Shoving the unemployed into poverty.
Starving children.
Leaving the sick to die.
Jailing protesters.
Obstructing votes.

Whatever happened to our freedoms?

Ah, yes, of course,
they blew away with this latest storm.

Dislodged –
like our art and our education –
the unemployed and the uninsured –
our voices and our votes –
the unwanted and the minorities.

Then as now,
perpetrators cause these storms.
Not oddly, though –
the men and women of the earlier storm
did not present themselves as Christians.

ANOTHER TIME TODAY
Winter 2016

The plane swooped down –
thick clouds hid it above Bavaria.
For hours the crowd had waited –
fresh faced girls, innocent looking boys –
Dirndls and *Lederhosen*.
German flags and Swastikas.
The air rent asunder --
wild screams of the assembled.
The Austrian among Germans!
Der Führer!

The plane gracefully settled down –
clear mid-western sky.
They had watched him far up in the sky.
The crowd stood close to each other –
men and women,
old and young.
White faces above colorful attire.
Small and large American flags –
frenzied anticipation of Donald Trump.
Their hero had arrived.

The same slogans and lies,
as if our leaders had attended school
                              together then –
eighty years ago.
Slogans about renewing Germany:
Turn German blood pure again –
reverse losses imposed by Versailles –
undo Jewish ownership of the press –
remove foreigners from government
                                  and business.
Create jobs for men displaced
by the Depression and mechanical advances.

German industrialists kowtowing
                              to the *Führer*.

Slogans to make America Great again:
Unbind the decline accelerated by Obama,
that uppity black urbanite.
Deport murderous and raping Mexicans –
choke off the Jewish liberal press.
Appeal to workers displaced by innovation –
unable to catch on and catch up.
Political correctness trashed –
patriotic correctness held dear.
Corporate leaders kowtowing
to the adventurer.
Make America safe once more
for white Americans.

Lies were the currency two generations ago.
He said it well,
the master of the lie.
Joseph Goebbels was his name.
Hitler was his boss.
The bigger the lie, he uttered,
the more likely they will believe it.
Lies,
gaining currency once more.
Values and truths –
tweeted, twittered, and twisted away;
tattered by disciples of the master of the lie.

Expect the government to be the same
as the one –
then –
two full generations ago.

THE SYCOPHANT
Spring and Winter 2016

Yes, Sir!
What a profound statement!
How did you think of this?
You are so ingenuous!
We will carry out the implications.

Ah, yes, Madam!
What a brilliant idea!
How was it that you thought of it?
We will place the concept right now!

You were there with Egypt's pharaohs.
You surrounded the mighty Mongol lords.
You served the emperors of Rome.
You kowtowed to the great Ashoka.

You were there with Henry VIII –
and with his many wives.
You changed your opinions as often
as he the colors of his cloaks.
You were there for Elizabeth I
and her royal whims and ambitions.

You surrounded Peter I of Russia –
and applauded his abuses with platitudes.
You prided yourself for assisting Washington –
and from a distance watched his decline.

You genuflected before the latest Pope –
you saluted the most recent president –
however corrupt he, or she, might have been.

You never refused a largess:
Large estates, noble titles, military orders,
willing mistresses, excellent food,
                            and knowing smiles.

A sycophant's reward for being obsequious.

Yes, I was one.
How I desired being observed –
as I arrived with the august!
I was part of the entourage –
a puffed-up loyal member of the team.

Now it is too late to undo --
the corruption of my spirit and my soul.
Like all those beholden to any and all regimes –
I gloried in the golden rays of the powerful.

Hurrah! Hurrah!
The king is dead!
Long live the king!

SLOGAN-MAKERS
In Honor of Lillian Nave
Late Fall 2017

To followers,
slogans offer encouragement and hope;
saviors, those who craft them.
To others,
slogans produce astonishment and rejection;
ignorant of their uncanny appeal.

Hidden meanings clear to those who know.
Deutschland über Alles.
Germany above all.
Read: *Deutsche über Alle.*
Germans above all Others.
Make America great again.
Read: *Make white America great again.*
Nazi followers dream:
a reunited Germany –
      no more Jewish journalism,
           Gypsy stealing,
                gay perversion.
American admirers hope:
another America –
    no more Black power,
        Mexican labor,
           gay perversion,
                Muslim prayer.
German leaders planned for Jews in Madagascar,
they designed instead –
the horror of the concentration camps.
American leaders deride African Americans –
they force Mexicans back to Mexico –
they keep Muslims out of their "Christian" retreat –
and invade the bedrooms of their citizens.

Slogans –
means to an end:

Full-fledged and aspiring dictators –
expressing their desires.

Assisted by flags and teleprompters –
sycophants whispering and admirers defending.

Those not in the know --
creating explanations removed from reality --
seeing men and women left behind and disillusioned.

Power, the authoritarians' aim –
the naive who place them there,
not their concern.

GLORIOUS NATION/S
Winter 2016

The best.
The very best.
Better than the very best.
The greatest.
The very greatest.
Far greater than the greatest.
The most successful.
The most successful ever.
The most significant.
The most significant of all times.

Beyond imagination,
brilliant, powerful, privileged.
Never before such men and women –
and places.
All meant to endure forever.
All destroyed from within.

Shang's China;
Ashoka's India;
Rameses II's Egypt;
Augustus' Rome;

Kublai Khan's Mongolia;
Montezuma's Aztek Empire;
Peter the First's Russia;
Hitler's *Third Reich*;
Stalin's Soviet Union.
And our beloved USA?

Emperors, kings, and pharaohs;
presidents, prime ministers, and leaders.
Arrogant and self-absorbed;
power hungry and mad for success.
Political hacks and maneuverers –
yes-men and sycophants –
present in every palace.

Family greed and corporate malfeasance –
noble privileges in a different form.
Warlords, knights, and generals –
brilliants and killers by different names.
Human and natural resources
wasted for a privileged few –
slavery and poverty but collateral damage.

Religious supporters and crusaders –
the long-standing tradition never to be ignored.
Education attempted and abandoned –
access to privilege only for the few.

Nothing taught –
nothing learned.
None ever ready for the end.

*Photo of Caesar Augustus, better known as Emperor Augustus.

AUTHORITARIANS ON THE RISE
In Memory of Dietrich Bonhoeffer
Fall 2017

The last major war illustrated it:
The authoritarians' approach is not viable.

Democracies hesitatingly spread across the globe.
But –
Stalin still in charge in the Soviet Union,
Mao Zedong's brutal excesses in China, and
millions leaving from Eastern Europe and India.

Alliances and counter-alliances –
peace flourished again across the world.
Trade and commerce without borders.

Living standards on the rise.

The countertrend –
70 years in the making:
Compromise a waste time,
processes take far too long.
Flexibility one of the casualties.

New leaders avoid compromise and arguments;
quick solutions in vogue again.
A new tone prevails –
in universities, high schools,
corporations,
and in churches.
People genuflect –
advocate for poor decisions.
Authoritarians hold sway again.

Firings a routine –
following confrontations.

*The photograph of Dietrich Bonhoeffer; available on Wikipedia.

A PIG'S BEAUTIFUL BODY
*In Honor of Ken Fuchsman
Summer 2014*

Little pig –
on the side of the street –
on a wooden crate –
in the blistering sun.
Barely covered at the top –
naked at the bottom –
like a woman raped.
Dead in mid-town Manhattan.

A barbecue feast –
about to happen up the street.

You grew up far away –
in the countryside.
Innocent and unsuspecting –
intelligent and yet unaware –
your cruel fate never revealed.

Not seeing the massive stacks of wood
about to roast you like St. Lawrence long ago.

Your tender skin –
bruised and charred –
your body handled and torn.
Hungry gawkers seeing juicy morsels –
where you had been –
the living being.

Displayed on cheap paper plates –
enhanced by plastic condiments
and yellow beer and brownish coke.

All gulped down by carnivores –
the remnants consumed on the ground

by overstuffed dogs –
unaware of their fellow creature's end.

You prided yourself on your magnificent body.
The revelers saw nothing more than a piece of meat.
They were all about eating and drinking
at their street festival.

REFUGEES/ *FLÜCHTLINGE/ PROFUGHI*
In Memory of Those Who Did Not Survive
Fall 2015, Winter 2016

    They hide in forests,
    bobble in boats,
    press under fences,
    walk on stony paths,
    slog near concrete highways.
    They die on their way.
    Farmers, wives, shopkeepers, mothers,
    teachers, barbers, daughters, priests,
    merchants, masons, healers,
    brothers, husbands, and sons.

    Young and old –
    rich and poor –
    all forced away.

    Threadbare clothing on emaciated bodies –
    hands struggling with bare essentials.
    Faces filled with misery.

HOPES AND FEARS

Fear of greater catastrophe in every move –
yet hoping for a better future.

Millions upon millions –
driven from hearth and home –
from tiny plots into arms of strangers.

Famine, war, conquest, death –
the dreaded horsemen of the past.
Add bigotry, extremism, hatred,
                        destruction, rape,
                                  torture, murder.
And call it terror.
Lust for power,
envy of success,
greed for more of the same,

pride in knowing more than others,
intolerance of difference.

They met them at home,
on their paths,
and in their potential home.
Hundreds of years in the past,
decades ago,
today.
Monarchs, tyrants, and dictators of the past,
fanatics, politicians, and crooks of the present –
enhancing humanity's plight,
ruining chances of a peaceful life.

Little understanding of loss and pain.
Mostly meanness –
pure and simple,
and lack of love.

HISTORY SHOULD TEACH US DIFFERENTLY
In Memory of Those Killed by Dictators
Winter 2017

History teaches lessons to those
                      who would oppress.
They manipulate,
        devalue,
                imprison,
                        and murder.

Eager to hear the siren call of charmers.
Abused childhoods and failed adulthoods!

Weakened resistance to those --
gleefully absorbed with themselves
and ready to abuse this weakness.

Were it –
history taught us differently!

BEDTIME STORIES
In Memory of Helene and Ferdinand Wittine
February 2018

She told them to the little girl when she came to visit.
A past dragged into the present --
one generation to the other.

Back then, in Yugoslavia,
she began.
Then, when the war raged between
                                   Germans and Partisans* –
she and her husband lived between the two sides.

In the hairdresser's studio,
wives and girlfriends told of the coming attack.
Right there in front of her:
Their men would surprise the German army.

The women did not suspect her
of understanding every word.
She sat there motionless, her face a mask.
She did not want to collapse,
along with her husband,
bullets tearing at their bodies.

She did not know then:
The women knew her all too well;
her husband translated for their men.

A few nights later, she said,
the Partisans walked by the house.
Their weapons clanked and they spoke without restraint.
She laid in bed frightened,
clinging to her husband.
The man who cooperated with the enemy.

Granddaughter huddled stiffly below her sheets –
fear chasing away pleasant childhood dreams.

PRESCIENCE

When grandmother spoke again,
she told of many German soldiers in a cave –
walled in by heavy rocks.
The Partisans did not reveal their location.
If her husband knew, he did not tell.

The girl under the featherbed burdened
it seemed by heavy rocks.

She read about it in the paper decades later:
The German soldiers almost made it –
buried alive,
their skeletons
found in their tattered uniforms.

In gilded palaces men look into mirrors,
seeing themselves in a narcissistic trance –
not seeing the faces of those others,
the ones they ordered maimed and murdered.

The pursuit of greater glory.

*The Partisans fought the German *Wehrmacht* in Yugoslavia during WWII.

DON'T FORGET
Fall 2013

Into massive openings –
one row of small fountains each –
pour streams of glistening water,
creating, like the Niagara,
an irresistible pull.

Relentlessly cascading
onto enormous platforms –
silver streams locked into one,
as if creating sheets of glass and steel.
Barely easing their descent,
they rush to further depths in their midst –
in search of the Towers' feet.

Soft clouds of mist
rise from each abyss,
spreading an uneven film
on the names of those who fell in September.
White roses here and there
marking birthdays that will never be again.

Off-course planes to those on the ground –
not hearing the screams inside.
Massive bombs approaching,
mostly unseen to those in the Twins –
not suspecting the unfolding tragedy.

They came from many lands,
the people in the Towers –
their work reaching around the globe.
One frantic call, one final note:
Good bye, my dear, good bye.
I must go now.
Down the stairs – never to be seen again.

PRESCIENCE

New Yorkers rushed in and up,
not knowing of the magnitude of harm –
mayhem beyond imagination –
attempting rescue where the finest barely could.
Their names reflecting ancestry and courage:
English,
    Italian,
        Polish,
            Jewish,
                Irish,
                    German,
                      Chinese.
Buried, all of them,
by the anger of the bombers –
flying to do them harm.
Not considering the hopes of others,
they murdered in a misinterpretation of their faith.

This is our martyrs' final resting place –
human beings, some not yet born,
having met their unwanted fate.

Don't forget them, America!
They died for you.

*The photograph was taken by the author
in August of 2015.

ADAM AND EVE
Winter 2017

Eve accepted –
the apple from the snake.
Adam took it;
it was too glorious not to take.

The teachers didn't say in school –
sex was the essence of this scene.
They taught instead:
Satan was the sneak.

The Bible reads:
Eve fell for this trick.

The men who wrote this text implied:
She offered her shiny skin.
They did not say:
BOTH gained knowledge of procreation.

HE was not pleased.
HE threw them out of HIS luscious garden.
HE made them manage on their own.

Men privileged their interpretation:
Men's revenge for women's naked skin!
Their power over women:
She sinned!

Time and time again –
they blamed her for their abuse.
They sold her,
they bought her,
they married her off,
they hid her in back rooms.

They dressed her from top to bottom.
Others should not see –
what they believed she would reveal,
thinking her all too eager --
to offer that famous apple once again.

Until now!
She is throwing the apple in his face:
"You took what was not yours to take."

*The image is of the oil painting "Adam and Eve" (1507), by Albrecht Dürer. [This work is in the public domain.]

AFTER US
In Honor of Samuel Scheffler
Winter and Summer 2014

Death –
I fear you.
I know your work;
you took my brother in infancy.

I fear you,
Grim Reaper.
You will undo my thoughts, voice, and actions.
You take me from home and friends --
even life.

Yet –
fearsome harvester –
not even you bring complete finality.
Like my brother --
I will live on in the memory of others
until you harvest them as well.

Beyond that,
my works and grave will speak of my existence.

Within these realities –
lies my profoundest fear –
the thought of the disappearance of us all.
What indeed, if in thirty years
our entire species fell to your determination!
What if you took us all?

Then no one would –
read our poetry;
hear our music;
view our art;
inhabit our buildings;
taste our foods;
not even drink our water.

No one would rediscover –
our thoughts, our efforts, our creations –
even our gravestones.
All – gone forever!

Grim Reaper!
Would there be a record of our presence
without our presence?

And, tell us, Mighty Lord,
would the journey of our souls' continue?

No, I fear,
they would be *gone* as well –
for they too are human constructs.

*Samuel Scheffler, *Death and the Afterlife*, edited by Niko Kolodny, commentaries by Susan Wolf, Harry G. Frankfurt, Seana Valentine Shiffrin and Niko Kolodny. (New York & London: Oxford University Press, 2013).

CONCLUSION

Every one of us constantly rewrites his or her personal history, our story. We want to assure ourselves that it makes sense to us and, hopefully, to others. I have written mine first in scholarly formats, in a play, a novel, and most recently, in poetry. The inspiration for this latest rendition of my story stems from Patrick Modiano's introduction to Francoise Frenkel, *Nichts, um sein Haupt zu betten* [trans. from the French *Rien ou poser sa tete* (1945/2018) by Elisabeth Edel (Munich: btb, 2018)]. Modiano writes (p. 8) that sometimes we discover a text or experience a moment, like a conversation in a train compartment long ago, that changes us forever. For him, Frenkel's *No Place to Lay One's Head* was such a book.

For me, such a change came with the violent death of Winnetou, Karl May's famous American-Indian hero. My reading of this fictional calamity preceded the demise of my grandfather by a few weeks. In my recollections, the death of the Apache Chief left a greater impact than that of my grandfather. The simple reason remains that May's famous volumes about Redskins (!) and white cowboys and rail-roaders were my first exposure to novels.

Up to then, novels had not been part of my life. There were no books either on the farm in the Dolomite Mountains in Northern Italy, where I grew up, nor in the monastery schools, which I had attended there.

The impact of this novel was enhanced because I had entered the excitement of two faraway places: one was West Germany's Rhineland where my grandfather lived, and the other the supposed homeland of the Native American. Even if the latter did not reflect many real places or real Indians, or fights between them, the cowboys and the railroad men, the descriptions left an indelible impression.

Let me add: Winnetou had not been my first hero. In the monasteries we had already built bridges with Caesar in Gaul (in Latin) and reveled in the exploits of Odysseus and Xenophon (in Greek).

However, the exposure to the late 19th century German author was different. Sitting in a chair in my grandfather's living room, with books behind me and beside me, I felt safe and could

bemoan without inhibition the unexpected death of my new hero... Bitter
tears flowed for days. This was an outpouring that may have been connected to the age of my grandfather. To this then twelve-year-old, he was ancient and near death. Yet, in the short time we knew each other in person; Kurt Dalmer became my walking partner and storyteller about WWI, the Depression, and the bombing raids during WWII.

His death soon after Winnetou's demise surprised us, and it changed our world. My mother and my aunt sold their parental home in Krefeld-Uerdingen, leaving my mother and me without a home. My mother had to move into a small apartment and to work, soon opening a cosmetology salon.

I went off to monastery school, once more. The reflection about the fictional Winnetou, and the comfort of reading in my grandfather's space, explains my life-long fascination with the written word, having access to it and working with it. When I left for the U.S. in 1957, the plan was for me to work in factories, or at best in an office, but the education I brought from Italy and Germany discouraged such a career path. Factory or office work meant a life without books and life without books meant, even to me as a teenager, life without something essential.

There is no straight line between Odysseus, Xenophon, Caesar, Winnetou and the desire to continue and complete my education; but the meandering led to a Ph.D. in NYU's evening school. After reaching this goal, I started as a faculty member at Appalachian State University in Boone, NC in 1968.

When my father's stint in the SS entered my consciousness, less than ten years later, I refined the skill already gained in writing to clarify my thinking; I wrote and wrote, and then wrote some more.

When I endeavored, in retirement, to both explain and leave the paternal authoritarian, new forms of writing became tools of choice. Most recently, after a play and a novel, poetry offers the sharp succinctness and emotional depth that none of other written expressions offered.

NOTES

FATHER AND MOTHER
First published in Peter Petschauer (2014), *In the Face of Evil. The Sustenance of Tradition* (pp. xi-xii). Charleston, SC: Perspektiven Presse.

THREE MOTHERS, PLUS ONE
First published in Peter Petschauer (2014), *In the Face of Evil. The Sustenance of Tradition* (p. 271). Charleston, SC: Perspektiven Presse.

ATTILA, FENCER, JEW
Published in *Clio's Psyche,* 22(3), 160-164. (2014, December.) Republished in David Beisel (Ed.) (2016), *Wounded Centuries. A Selection of Poems* (p. 47). Nyack, NY: Circumstantial Productions/ Cambridge, MA: Grolier Poetry Press.

MY HOLOCAUST
Published in David Beisel (Ed.) (2016), *Wounded Centuries. A Selection of Poems* (pp. 49-50). Nyack, NY: Circumstantial Productions/Cambridge, MA: Grolier Poetry Press.

BACK INTO THE FUTURE
Published in *Clio's Psyche*, 22(3), 160-164. (2015, December.) Republished in David Beisel (Ed.) (2016), *Wounded Centuries. A Selection of Poems* (pp. 51-52). Nyack, NY: Circumstantial Productions/ Cambridge, MA: Grolier Poetry Press.

OUR DEAD ARE WITH US FOREVER
Published in *Clio's Psyche*, 21(1), 19-20. (2014, June.) Republished in David Beisel (Ed.) (2016), *Wounded Centuries. A Selection of Poems* (pp. 48-49). Nyack, NY: Circumstantial Productions/ Cambridge, MA: Grolier Poetry Press.

FRANZ HERDA, AMERICAN-GERMAN
Published in *Clio's Psyche*, 22(4), 268-269. (2016, Winter.)

TOWARD THE END, APRIL 1945
Published in *Clio's Psyche,* 22(3), 160-164. (2015, December.)

THE SYCOPHANT
Published in *Clio's Psyche*, 24(1), 23-24. (2017, Summer.)

GLORIOUS NATION/S
Published in *Clio's Psyche*, 23(2), 191-192. (2017, Winter.)

DON'T FORGET
Published in David Beisel (Ed.) (2016), *Wounded Centuries. A Selection of Poems* (pp.52-53). Nyack, NY: Circumstantial Productions/Cambridge, MA: Grolier Poetry Press.

ADAM AND EVE
Published in *Clio's Psyche*, 25 (1), 32-33. (2018, Fall.)

www.ingramcontent.com/pod-product-compliance
Lightning Source LLC
Chambersburg PA
CBHW070542170426
43200CB00011B/2519